A strikingly noticeable feature of this simple woman, is her pleasant countenance. A friendly smile is always on her face, a sparkling glow emerges from her droopy eyes, and her word is comforting and hugs reassuring. I am stunned and curious about her ambitions in life, the secret behind her austere composure, the driving force for her success. "I am no superstar actress, renowned model, or convincing politician", she reminds me. It is this obscure, yet productive individual, who, fortunately, I was able to meet in three separate environments. She is a mother of four young, energetic boys, a wife of a medical doctor, a Principal for a private school. I wonder how she ostensibly effortlessly accomplishes each of these very different, difficult tasks, still maintaining a cheerful disposition.

"It is sometimes tiresome", she informs me, "to fulfill four obligations in one lifetime." She smirks and adds, "However, the satisfaction is worth all my effort." I guess that hidden within her claim of personal satisfaction, there was another motivation which I was expected to know. My first analysis of her character, coming from her home activities, is her efficiency. She performs duties of a mother, wife and maid here. "My home is my family, my kids are foremost responsibility. I don't hire helpers or babysitters, because I want to be involved with my family and to provide for them." Contrary to my belief, the atmosphere definitely appeared clean and well maintained. I soon learned that "laundry and dusting are daily tasks," and for someone so occupied with other obligations, she even had time to spare to speak to me. Even more astounding is this woman's proficiency at work. I assume from her humility that a Principal's position is no easier than that of a teacher. She demands nothing- only requests that everyone "participates and follows the schedule." Her students respect her, try to never disappoint her and use her successful life as their model. Being a private school, funds are more in demand, and I discovered from the community that the extra green bills come secretly. What drives such unrewarding charitable deeds? What supplies the energy to withstand the monotony of everyday life? How does one fulfill three entirely different responsibilities with such perfection? "Things are not all so easy and opportunities do not just come darting towards me. Looks could be very deceiving, my dear!"

I did not expect such a negative response from my hero, one who I hoped to befriend. However, through this significant revelation, I learnt a life-molding lesson. "Life is always what you make it to be. It could be disastrous because of that one and only big mistake, or pleasing as a result of a that right decision or correct guiding path." It is belief in punishments and rewards in the afterlife that spurs her on- her religion. Despite being infamous, her contributions influence everything. This great young woman is Leslie Polnifax-Abolfathi. Familiar scenes gush into my memory with every visit to my old, dilapidated home. I always fail to disguise my presence, even if I approach the 2-foot, crouched, crowded doorway, on the very tips of my toes. Mother always greets me her outstretched arms clamp around my panting, heaving chest, and, with her tight, suffocating embrace, she tilts her head, raises an eyebrow and with concerned direct words, she questions about my day. I try to wiggle and squirm to freedom. Ultimately, my sweaty, frigid palms grasp her circling arms, and fling her aside. Endeavoring to force a smile through my gritted teeth, I look away, and, with my head hanging and stuttering words, I manage to ask the contents of dinner. Only then, would the fresh, spicy aroma of food reach my leaking, stuffy nostrils. For the first time since my arrival home, I deeply inhale, my bony ribs jutting out forming a scrubbing board. With my eyes shut tight, I reminisce over past days. My own private canopy is my rescue from life's unfortunate vicissitudes. The four whitewashed walls protect me literally from outside dangers.

It is here where I frequently sprawl and stare into the black nothingness of the night; here I muster my energy, through sleep, to face another frantic day; here, my personality, my beliefs is revealed. This 'prison' is truly the avenue through which I vent my emotions. The walls support my reminders for the next day and are adorned with favorite family photos. The Bathroom, A place always occupied when I must use it. The door is scared with niches from pounding fists and kicking feet, aimed at prying it open. It is the one room, which our entrance is so necessary, and our exit, determined by the extent of the outside hair-raising threats. The final room for which I have delightful memories is the one - where, as a one-unit family, we share something special. Its aura, at times, seems to intensify my guilty verdicts.

Only the clock is swinging a pendulum breaks the silence: the dim, dusty, cobweb bulbs indicates everyone's mood: and strewn tattered, soiled clothing display our mental confusion. Despite the untidy, bleak, musty atmosphere, we all experience a joy unfelt by many whose abode may be more luxurious than ours. Somehow, as we all huddle around the short, cracked, unstable table, the air seems cleaner, the lit room, brighter and our feelings uplifted. Moreover, this is where my memory fades as Dad enters the room. He grumbles and stumbles across the kitchen. We all try to be neater in our appearance- I sit erect, gather my strangling hair into a single pony and place the broadest possible smile on my face. As we again sit together, the familiar emotion arises. With no dinner formalities holding us back, other than our daily thanksgiving prayer, we insert our utensils into the cold Spaghetti. The glistening bright rays of the sun decline and seems to say, "Your seeing each other tomorrow is not guaranteed--as my rising. "Appreciate every moment together, for nothing always lasts!" Concealing our emotions in order to avoid shame may prove more embarrassing when the truth is comes out. However, frankly expressing our innermost opinions could also initiate that 'dreaded' disapproval. Predicaments, which may cause such thoughts to develop, arise more frequently within the family than any other social institution. Speaking to a 'perfect' person, at an appropriate time, with carefully selected words is ideal. However, to many, such opportunities are rare, resulting in us turning to secrecy, lies and pretense to evade hurt. What should be our approach? Each dilemma could be resolved with one simple act. In my situation, I was different, abnormal in that I did not share similar views as others in my generation- within my family and socially. It was from this incident that I acquired significant lessons, which still affect my approach to all problems. My earliest memories consist mainly of fear and shame the constant fear of disagreeing with certain norms and rules of my time shame to dispute anyone's commands and voice my own opinion. Mendacity became habitual, followed by an overwhelming feeling of guilt. I began living a double standard. At certain times I was myself, at others, a person whom I was expected to be. Whatever I expected others wanted me to say, I professed.

Whatever was I asked of me I did. I surrendered unconditionally and immediately to the demands, expectations and assumptions of my family simultaneously withdrawing into a world known only to me and which I was too timid to expose. The world I so cautiously hid was one in which I made the rules- there were none! I was free to embrace all opportunities I liked. It was here in my mind's world that I envisioned a realization that got me into the character I am today. I slowly noticed that being evasive when questioned about my views, only produced an---eternal circle of deceit. Sometimes, one may forget the lies and ends up constructing more lies to cover up the original. I concluded that frankness and maintaining a firm stance from the very beginning, is much safer although difficult.

We feel the insecurity of losing a friend's or loved one's affection and acceptance of tainting our image. We want to state our emotions but are uncertain if it is right. It was the conflicting feelings that caused me to search the intention of all my actions, these fluctuating thoughts, that constantly nibbled my mind and coerced me into facing reality. By meticulously selecting words, I attempted to explain and display the true me. Although I faced the discrimination and rejection I so cautiously avoided, I gained personal contentment. At least I did not now have to disguise myself under the cloak of "the perfect, normal child". In light of my particular experience, I have concluded that honest, controlling conversation is the key to the lock of people's heart.

The door of acceptance is normally wedged, if individuals hold contrasting views, and is even harder to open if one is adamant and antagonistic in his own view. Refraining from aggression does not mean we automatically comply with the other's opinion. It is a form of respect and ultimately an advantage to win our opponent. With this, I revealed my inner beauty. With some, I have earned respect, even admiration. "To be ignorant of one's ignorance is the malady of the ignorant..." There are few people with enough humility to take constructive criticisms and change. I have learnt that arrogance causes us to become angry if wrong or when corrected. Now I try to investigate myself and be aware of my faults, so I would be in a much better position to determine whether any change is necessary on my part.

Man generally seeks to please man rather than self, and if he does please himself, it is to such an extreme that it becomes selfishness. I have chosen the intermediate course, of doing what I know is right, regardless of others' remarks. In this way, I acquire personal inner peace. Neither is it easy to undergo persecution because of general differences of opinions. Although society's insularity may seem to remove our attempts to be unique. We should take the difficult route of being true to ourselves, bravely and with patient perseverance. I rest my point, with a quotation of Pope John Paul -- "An honest man is the noblest work of God." Some say success is how well we perform at certain activities. How could we truly succeed here in this life, overcoming all obstacles in our constant strife?

Is success worldwide recognition and monetary gain? On the other hand, is it simply conquering setbacks and dauntlessly facing our pain? Is it reserved only for those who are considered renowned and mighty? Could it really be achieved with available opportunity? Who should grade us and tell us what is our best? After failing once, could we ever progress? For me, success comes when I make others happy. Duties of a student, a daughter, a sister, a friend Success are how I feel when my day is at its end. During my short life, and through it is many vicissitudes. I have learned the true definition of success. Most of us want the successful status, a prominent position, and the applauded work. We measure success by the amount of money we make, the number of degrees we attain, the size of our house, the model of our cars, the external beauty of our spouses. We may equate materialistic gain to success and this type of success to true happiness. Nevertheless, could we honestly declare that wealth, not character, lightens our burdens or that the rich have many consolations? Prevalent around us, we could easily identify explicit, notable images of success a Harvard graduate; an acquired job raise; heroic rescues extraordinary, flexible gymnastic movements. But concealed by the glimmer of such celebrated headlines, lies. Another aspect of success the everyday subtle acts which affect greatly on those receiving them. A kind smile, encouraging words, even consoling hugs go a long way in assisting depressed, distraught individuals. By simply posing a friendly disposition, one may indeed lessen the intensity of a strained social condition. When around strangers, why hang your head, dart your eyes away, and pretend to ignore their presence? I am not proposing that success include clowning about, using extreme flattery and giggling foolishly around others. I humbly suggest that maintaining a pleasant appearance, despite our grueling burdens, is truly admirable and although neglected by many, these gracious acts may make us successful by the end of our day. It is only through overcoming arrogance and fostering humility that we are able to appreciate honest critics and ultimately succeed. It is quite a feat, to identify one's faults and acknowledge the necessity for change. Although some pride may be lost when we admit our guilt, we would certainly gain the respect of intelligent people, who are able to recognize our efforts to improve.

Such respect may even develop into a 'successful' friendship, whereby each person learns intellectual lessons in successfully approach life. Success also comes from acquiring knowledge, not just receiving an education. I agree that certificates, degrees and medals represent our successful acquisition of specific information or accomplished feats. We tend to rid our haughty emotions. Becoming educated forces us to meet those with more experience than ourselves, and this motivates us to succeed in learning more. Every step, with which we cautiously take to reach our ambition, we are sure to encounter hampering obstacles. Repetitious failure may dampen that initial drive to succeed. I believe that only from failure can we really know what it feels like to achieve. Success is learning from one's mistakes, yet clinging to that which is virtuous and helpful. It is gathering our strength to get up, focusing on our specific dream, reorganizing our strategy and facing the obstacle again. It is appreciating the reality that we "cannot have our cake and eat it as well!" Success is the result of determination despite our frequent collisions with discouraging drawbacks. My theory of success emerged from analyzing the characters of those whom I admire and people who are widely renowned. Did distinguished actors attain such a position without exhaustedly weary efforts? In fact, unless we are fortunate' to be the offspring of Royalty, or an heir to fortunes, everyone who is considered rich, somewhere in their life, worked hard without quitting. If we even desire an iota of success, we should marvel over their efforts and follow the footsteps of productive exemplars.

Whether one ponders over these suggestions or blindly plunges into the guileful approach, keep in mind that success of any type comes only after hard work. All of us creep before we can walk, and walk before we learn to run. We all begin life as unrecognized nobodies, then strive to achieve the spectacular impression display. We may be born into a successful family, come from a successful school, or be around successful people. This does not guarantee us personal success. Although achievement maybe reached through a variety of avenues, three factors are common and essential: hard work through discipline, persistent efforts despite failure and realistic goals set by personal motivation and not the pressuring expectations of others. Death dying extinction. These words conger images of grief, suffering and, sometimes old age.

In this life, we are all guaranteed to die- is it in war, an accident, or simply fatigue. Death strikes at all, regardless of our financial status, family royalty or race. It will happen to a parent, sibling and a friend. Experiencing such trauma in one's life may cause us to wish that our loved ones never died. However, what would the affairs of a world relay be like, if all life were eternal? I shall define death as a procedure that removes us from this 'real' world. What if there was no such thing as dying or death for all creatures? I imagine the world to be an entirely different place. There would definitely be no need for religion, since this tries to console us, prepare us, and even explain to us about the nature of death. Moreover, if death does not occur, then what will be the purpose of religion?

Consequently, without this guiding path in life, there would follow a complete dilapidation of morals and ethics in the human race. Everyone will now try to acquire as much worldly possessions as possible; in order to make this long life comfortable after all it is going to be a very long life! No one, or a very few percentage, will think about doing good and being kind, etc., etc. If this is our one and only life, then why should anyone do a "righteous deeds"? With this mentality, I see one of two calamities occurring a complete rejection or disintegration of all religious systems, or an entirely new evolution of religion. A painless death of course, but just a rescue from the hardship of life. I guess there will also be an increase in the number of diseases. Death virtually removes certain unfit, unable sections of society.

Without it, not only people, but also all living things will just continue consuming the resources of the earth, and their productions. Since nature must run its course in terms of preparing generations for better survival, I see that people will develop physical features, unknown to us today. That is, there will be a change or evolution in certain aspects of our appearance. We will age more slowly; thus looking a particular age would differ drastically. I imagine my peers, at age forty, with skin of fifteen-year-olds. This may cause social havoc, and even inferiority complexes, as we try to maintain our "good looks". Indeed, there will be a great demand on the cosmetic industry to provide a remedy of totally stopping the aging process. No death means that there would be no need for cemeteries and cremation sites. Whew!

This would be great, since this provides a lot more land space for the now ever increasing population. There will be a birth to death ratio of 100:0, which implies infinity! I am positive that society will embark to enforce birth control laws, trying to limit the population increase to a certain extent. I do not believe this would help though, because if no one dies then no one should be born in order to keep the ratio equal. This is an impossible feat. So no death means a heightened demand in land space, sky space, even "space." A removal of burial will provide a solution, temporarily. There would be an increase in the number a people living in a single area, all compacted, like sardines in a can. A more adjacent world, probably even a universal language, shared concerns a literally smaller world.

If no death occurs, nothing will become extinct. Consequently, there would be no need for museums. Well, probably these institutions will now display creatures in their youthful stage, before evolution, showing their appearance before they developed features for better survival. Finally, I envision a forever-constant battle for power, position, and wealth. An increase in the demand of jobs may result in many people being unemployed or always remaining in the position, say, Assistant Manager. This leads to an increase in crimes like theft. One good will emerges, and that is the eradication of all murders, suicides and homicides. However, people will start inventing other methods to "get rid off" others, such as attacking with the intent to lame! Since we are all entitled to dream "what if" questions, I propose we think about

"What if we meet our deceased loved ones and live in an environment free from all bad?" Probably then we may find some consolation for our pain.

Sincerely;

Sir. Faramarz Fred Abolfathi

www.ingramcontent.com/pod-product-compliance
Lightning Source LLC
Chambersburg PA
CBHW051226170526

45166CB00005B/2068